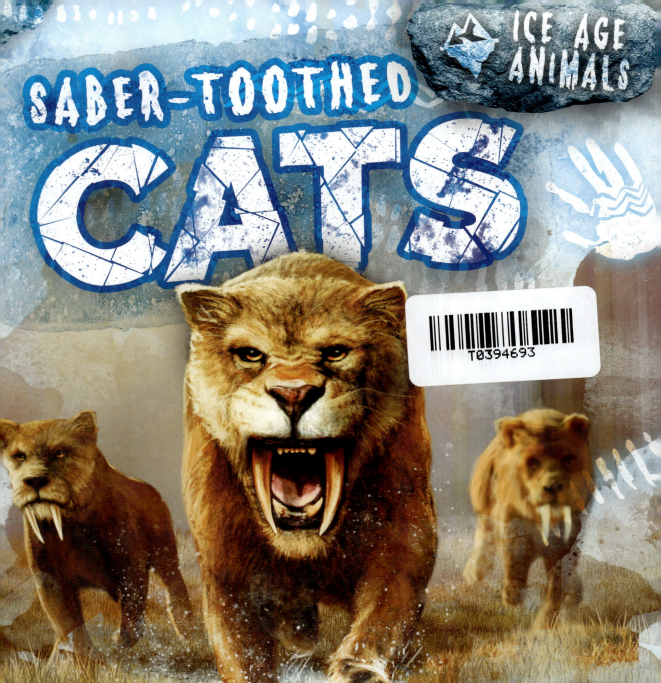

SABER-TOOTHED CATS

ICE AGE ANIMALS

BY ELIZABETH NEUENFELDT
ILLUSTRATIONS BY MAT EDWARDS

BELLWETHER MEDIA • MINNEAPOLIS, MN

EPIC

EPIC BOOKS are no ordinary books. They burst with intense action, high-speed heroics, and shadows of the unknown. Are you ready for an Epic adventure?

This edition first published in 2025 by Bellwether Media, Inc.

No part of this publication may be reproduced in whole or in part without written permission of the publisher. For information regarding permission, write to Bellwether Media, Inc., Attention: Permissions Department, 6012 Blue Circle Drive, Minnetonka, MN 55343.

Library of Congress Cataloging-in-Publication Data

Names: Neuenfeldt, Elizabeth, author. | Edwards, Mat, 1966- illustrator.
Title: Saber-toothed cats / by Elizabeth Neuenfeldt ; [illustrated by Mat Edwards].
Description: Minneapolis, MN : Bellwether Media, 2025. | Series: Epic : Ice age animals |
Includes bibliographical references and index. | Audience: Ages 7-12 | Audience: Grades 2-3 |
Summary: "Engaging images accompany information about saber-toothed cats. The combination of high-interest subject matter and light text is intended for students in grades 2 through 7"-- Provided by publisher.
Identifiers: LCCN 2024019777 (print) | LCCN 2024019778 (ebook) | ISBN 9798893040432 (library binding) | ISBN 9798893041620 (paperback) | ISBN 9781644879832 (ebook)
Subjects: LCSH: Saber-toothed tigers--Juvenile literature.
Classification: LCC QE882.C15 N48 2025 (print) | LCC QE882.C15 (ebook) | DDC 569/.75--dc23/eng/20240430
LC record available at https://lccn.loc.gov/2024019777
LC ebook record available at https://lccn.loc.gov/2024019778

Text copyright © 2025 by Bellwether Media, Inc. EPIC and associated logos are trademarks and/or registered trademarks of Bellwether Media, Inc. Bellwether Media is a division of Chrysalis Education Group.

Editor: Betsy Rathburn   Designer: Jeffrey Kollock

Printed in the United States of America, North Mankato, MN.

TABLE OF CONTENTS

WHAT WERE SABER-TOOTHED CATS?	4
THE LIVES OF SABER-TOOTHED CATS	10
FOSSILS AND EXTINCTION	16
GET TO KNOW THE SABER-TOOTHED CAT	20
GLOSSARY	22
TO LEARN MORE	23
INDEX	24

WHAT WERE SABER-TOOTHED CATS?

canine teeth

Saber-toothed cats were fearsome **predators**. They were known for their long, sharp **canine teeth**!

SABER-TOOTHED CAT RANGE MAP

EARTH

● = range

WHEN
First appeared during the Miocene epoch

WHAT BIG TEETH!
Some saber-toothed cat canines were 8 inches (20 centimeters) long!

There were many **species**. The first appeared around 16 million years ago. This was during the **Miocene epoch**.

5

Saber-toothed cats had furry coats. This likely helped them hide in their **habitats**.

furry coat

A FURRY MYSTERY

Scientists think saber-toothed cats that lived in forests had spotted coats. Saber-toothed cats in grassy areas likely had plain coats.

They had short tails. They had big feet and strong legs. They could **retract** their sharp claws!

Saber-toothed cats had strong bodies. They came in different sizes. The largest species were nearly 4 feet (1.2 meters) tall at the shoulders.

THE LIVES OF SABER-TOOTHED CATS

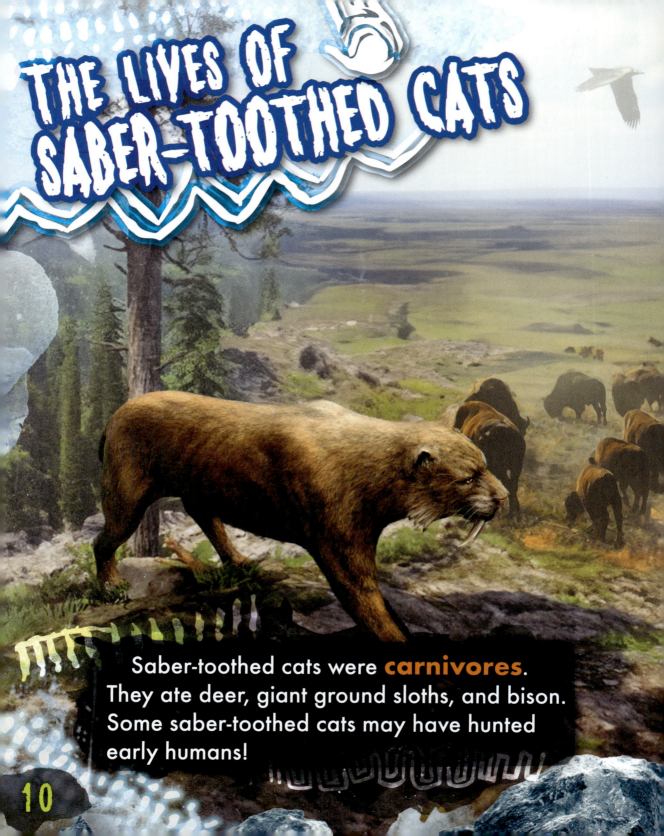

Saber-toothed cats were **carnivores**. They ate deer, giant ground sloths, and bison. Some saber-toothed cats may have hunted early humans!

SABER-TOOTHED CAT DIET

TYPE: carnivore

- deer
- giant ground sloths
- bison

They may have fought other predators for food.

Some saber-toothed cats **ambushed** their **prey**. Others chased their next meal.

Saber-toothed cats used their strong legs to **pounce** on their prey. They bit into meals with their long, **serrated** teeth.

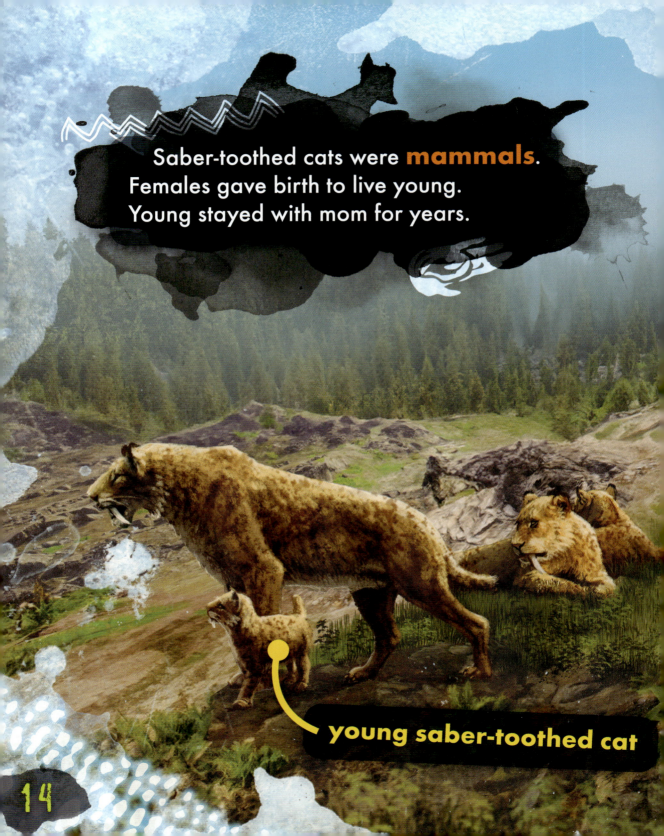

Saber-toothed cats were **mammals**. Females gave birth to live young. Young stayed with mom for years.

young saber-toothed cat

Saber-toothed cats may have lived in groups. They likely cared for sick or hurt group members.

FAMOUS FOSSIL FIND

WHEN: 2015

FOUND BY: Researchers from the Punta Hermengo Municipal Museum

FAMOUS FOR: First fossilized saber-toothed cat footprints

WHERE: Miramar, Argentina

SOUTH AMERICA

Around 10,000 years ago, many animals began going **extinct**. Saber-toothed cats could not find prey. They went extinct, too. People have found many saber-toothed cat **fossils**. They have even found footprints!

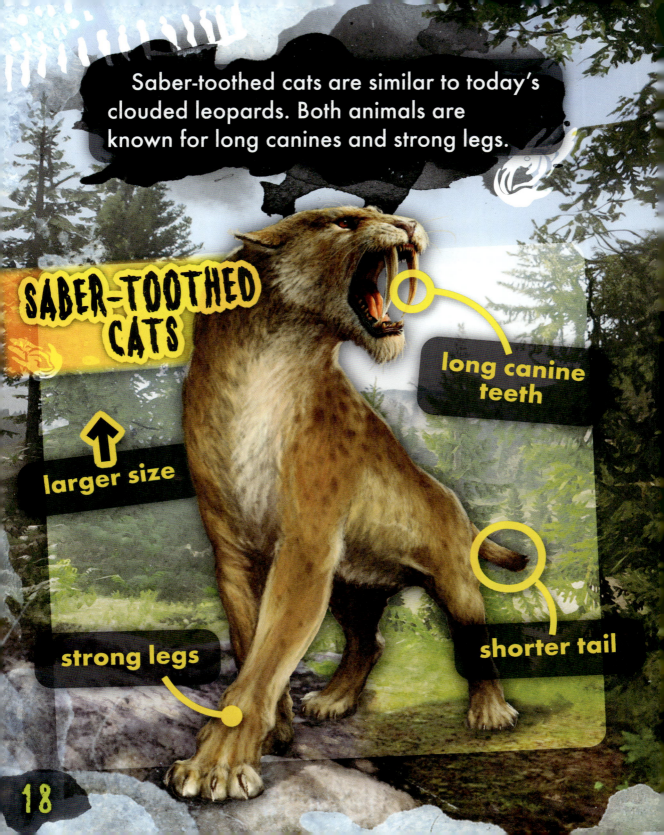

Saber-toothed cats are similar to today's clouded leopards. Both animals are known for long canines and strong legs.

SABER-TOOTHED CATS

- long canine teeth
- larger size
- shorter tail
- strong legs

CLOUDED LEOPARDS

- long canine teeth
- smaller size
- strong legs
- longer tail

Clouded leopards are smaller. Their tails are longer. Scientists can study them to learn more about saber-toothed cats!

GET TO KNOW THE SABER-TOOTHED CAT

WHO FIRST DESCRIBED A FOSSIL?
Peter Wilhem Lund in the **1840s**

short tail

strong legs

WEIGHT
= up to 900 pounds (408 kilograms)

DIET
deer
giant ground sloths
bison

20

GLOSSARY

ambushed—attacked from a hiding place

canine teeth—long, pointed teeth that are often the sharpest in the mouth

carnivores—animals that only eat meat

extinct—no longer living

fossils—the remains of living things that lived long ago

habitats—areas with certain types of plants, animals, and weather

mammals—warm-blooded animals that have backbones and feed their young milk

Miocene epoch—a geological time period that began around 23 million years ago and ended around 5.3 million years ago

pounce—to suddenly jump on something

predators—animals that hunt other animals for food

prey—animals that are hunted by other animals for food

retract—to pull back in

serrated—having a sawlike edge

species—types of animals

TO LEARN MORE

AT THE LIBRARY

Gish, Ashley. *Saber-toothed Cats*. Mankato, Minn.:
The Creative Company, 2023.

Hofer, Charles. *Siberian Tiger vs. Saber-tooth Cat*.
North Mankato, Minn.: Capstone Press, 2024.

Murray, Julie. *Saber-toothed Tiger*. Edina, Minn.:
ABDO, 2024.

ON THE WEB

FACTSURFER

Factsurfer.com gives you
a safe, fun way to find
more information.

1. Go to www.factsurfer.com.

2. Enter "saber-toothed cats" into the
   search box and click 🔍.

3. Select your book cover to see a list
   of related content.

INDEX

ambushed, 12

bodies, 8

canine teeth, 4, 5, 13, 18

carnivores, 10

claws, 7

clouded leopards, 18, 19

coats, 6, 7

diet, 11

extinct, 17

famous fossil find, 17

feet, 7

females, 14

food, 10, 11

footprints, 17

fossils, 17

get to know, 20–21

groups, 15

habitats, 6

legs, 7, 13, 18

mammals, 14

Miocene epoch, 5

predators, 4, 11

prey, 12, 13, 17

range map, 5

scientists, 7, 19

size, 5, 7, 8, 9, 19

species, 5, 8

tails, 7, 19

young, 14

The images in this book are reproduced through the courtesy of: Mat Edwards, front cover, pp. 4-5, 6-7, 8-9, 10-11, 12-13, 14-15, 16-17, 18-19, 20-21.